Two Modern Essays on Religion

A FREE MAN'S WORSHIP
by BERTRAND RUSSELL

THE FAITH OF A NATURALIST
by JOHN BURROUGHS

WESTHOLM PUBLICATIONS

HANOVER, NEW HAMPSHIRE

1959

To the Memory of
JOHN STUART MILL *and*
WILLIAM KILBORNE STEWART

Naturalism, the doctrine that religious truth is derived from nature, not revelation, has, since Spinoza, become a philosophy and a religion for many people

William Wordsworth was its poetic spokesman in the 19th century, and among thousands of others, he converted John Stuart Mill Furthermore, the impact of the ideas of Charles Darwin and Karl Marx, as well as the increase in the use of the scientific method, did much to moderate the orthodox faith of many

Today the teachings of orthodox Christianity are rejected by millions Two remarkable essays, which are not always easy to find, reflect this trend These are

1 A Free Man's Worship, by Bertrand Russell and

2 The Faith of a Naturalist, by John Burroughs, the great American naturalist who died in 1921

Both of these essays seem to me to face courageously some of the implications of the last two hundred years of scientific knowledge

Bertrand Russell wrote his A Free Man's Worship way back in 1903, when it first appeared in The Independent Review In a recent book edited by Paul Edwards and entitled Why I Am Not A Christian, issued in New York in 1957, Bertrand Russell agrees that, though he might not write the same essay today, he has never given up the naturalism implicit in many of the most famous passages of his remarkable essay

In 1927 he wrote "Fundamentally, my view of man's place in the cosmos remains unchanged I still believe that the major processes of the universe proceed according to the laws of physics, that they have no reference to our wishes, and are likely to involve the extinction of life on this planet, that there is no good reason for expecting life after death, and that good and evil are ideas which throw no light upon the non human world I still believe that, in times of moral difficulty and emotional stress, the attitude expressed in this essay is, at any rate for temperaments like my own, the one which gives most help in avoiding moral shipwreck"

If you read *The Faith of a Naturalist* by John Burroughs, you will see how far a naturalist has progressed from othodoxy since Henry Thoreau, who died in 1862 John Burroughs, who was a great American, and who was a symbol in his day of rugged Americanism, as Robert Frost is today, faced life with fortitude and courageously kept the integrity of his own mind His *Faith of a Naturalist*, which was printed in his book *Accepting the Universe*, is not always easy to find, so I am happy, as teacher and publisher, to present together these two famous essays, both for the use of my students and also for a few general readers

I am grateful to Houghton Mifflin Company, Boston, for permission to issue in an edition of 300 copies

John Burroughs' *The Faith of a Naturalist*, and also to
T Fisher Unwin of London for permission to reprint
Bertrand Russell's *A Free Man's Worship*.

HERBERT FAULKNER WEST
Professor of Comparative Literature
Dartmouth College, Hanover, N. H.
March, 1959

The Faith of A Naturalist

I

To say that man is as good as God would to most persons seem like blasphemy, but to say that man is as good as Nature would disturb no one Man is a part of Nature, or a phase of Nature, and shares in what we call her imperfections But what is Nature a part of, or a phase of?—and what or who is its author? Is it not true that this earth which is so familiar to us is as good as yonder morning or evening star and made of the same stuff?—just as much in the heavens, just as truly a celestial abode as it is? Venus seems to us like a great jewel in the crown of night or morning From Venus the earth would seem like a still larger jewel The heavens seem afar off and free from all stains and impurities of earth, we lift our eyes and our hearts to them as to the face of the Eternal, but our science reveals no body or place there so suitable for human abode and human happiness as this earth In fact, this planet is the only desirable heaven of which we have any clue Innumerable other worlds exist in the abysses of space which may be the abodes of beings superior, and of beings inferior, to ourselves We place our gods afar off so as to dehumanize them, never suspecting that when we do so we discount their divinity The more human we are,—remembering that to err is human,—the nearer God we are Of course good and bad are human concepts and are a verdict upon created things as they stand related to us, promoting or hindering our well-being In the councils of the Eternal there is apparently no such distinction

Man is not only as good as God, some men are a good deal better, that is, from our point of view, they attain a degree of excellence of which there is no hint in nature—moral excellence It is not until we treat man as a part of nature—as a product of the earth as literally as are the trees—that we can reconcile these contradictions If we could build up a composite man out of all the peoples of the earth, including even the Prussians, he would represent fairly well the God in nature

Communing with God is communing with our own hearts, our own best selves, not with something foreign and accidental Saints and devotees have gone into the wilderness to find God, of course they took God with them, and the silence and detachment enables them to hear the still, small voice of their own souls, as one hears the ticking of his own watch in the stillness of the night We are not cut off, we are not isolated points, the great currents flow through us and over us and around us, and unite us to the whole of nature Moses saw God in the burning bush, saw him with the eyes of early man whose divinities were clothed in the extraordinary, the fearful, or the terrible, we see him in the meanest weed that grows, and hear him in the gentle murmur of our own heart's blood The language of devotion and religious conviction is only the language of soberness and truth written large and aflame with emotion

Man goes away from home searching for the gods he carries with him always Man can know and feel and love only man There is a deal of sound psychology in the new religion called Christian Science—in that part which emphasizes the power of the mind over the body, and the fact that the world is largely what we make it, that evil is only the shadow of good—old truths reburnished This helps us to understand the hold it has taken upon such a large number of admirable persons Good and evil are relative terms, but evil is only the shadow of good Disease is a reality, but not in the same sense that health is a reality Positive and negative electricity are both facts, but positive and negative good belong to a different order Christian Science will not keep the distemper out of the house if the sewer-gas gets in, inoculation will do more to prevent typhoid and diphtheria than "declaring the truth" or saying your prayers or counting your beads In its therapeutical

3

value experimental science is the only safe guide in dealing with human corporal ailments

We need not fear alienation from God I feed Him when I feed a beggar I serve Him when I serve my neighbor I love Him when I love my friend I praise Him when I praise the wise and good of any race or time I shun Him when I shun the leper I forgive Him when I forgive my enemies I wound Him when I wound a human being I forget Him when I forget my duty to others If I am cruel or unjust or resentful or envious or inhospitable toward any man, woman, or child, I am guilty of all these things toward God "Inasmuch as ye have done it unto one of the least of these my brethren, ye have done it unto me"

II

I am persuaded that a man without religion falls short of the proper human ideal Religion, as I use the term, is a spiritual flowering, and the man who has it not is like a plant that never blooms The mind that does not open and unfold its religious sensibilities in the sunshine of this infinite and spiritual universe, is to be pitied Men of science do well enough with no other religion than the love of truth, for this is indirectly a love of God The astronomer, the geologist, the biologist, tracing the footsteps of the Creative Energy throughout the universe—what need has he of any formal, patent-right religion? Were

4

not Darwin, Huxley, Tyndall, and Lyell, and all
other seekers and verifiers of natural truth among the
most truly religious of men? Any of these men would
have gone to hell for the truth—not the truth of
creeds and rituals, but the truth as it exists in the
councils of the Eternal and as it is written in the laws
of matter and of life

For my part I had a thousand times rather have
Huxley's religion than that of the bishops who sought
to discredit him, or Bruno's than that of the church
that burnt him The religion of a man that has no
other aim than his own personal safety from some
real or imaginary future calamity, is of the selfish,
ignoble kind

Amid the decay of creeds, love of nature has high
religious value This has saved many persons in this
world—saved them from mammom-worship, and
from the frivolity and insincerity of the crowd It
has made their lives placid and sweet It has given
them an inexhaustible field for inquiry, for enjoy-
ment, for the exercise of all their powers, and in the
end has not left them soured and dissatisfied It has
made them contented and at home wherever they are
in nature—in the house not made with hands This
house is their church, and the rocks and the hills are
the altars, and the creed is written in the leaves of
the trees and in the flowers of the field and in the
sands of the shore A new creed every day and new

5

preachers, and holy days all the week through Every walk to the woods is a religious rite, every bath in the stream is a saving ordinance Communion service is at all hours, and the bread and wine are from the heart and marrow of Mother Earth There are no heretics in Nature's church, all are believers, all are communicants The beauty of natural religion is that you have it all the time, you do not have to seek it afar off in myths and legends, in catacombs, in garbled texts, in miracles of dead saints or wine-bibbing friars It is of to-day, it is now and here, it is everywhere The crickets chirp it, the birds sing it, the breezes chant it, the thunder proclaims it, the streams murmur it, the unaffected man lives it Its incense rises from the plowed fields, it is on the morning breeze, it is in the forest breath and in the spray of the wave The frosts write it in exquisite characters, the dews impearl it, and the rainbow paints it on the cloud It is not an insurance policy underwritten by a bishop or a priest, it is not even a faith, it is a love, an enthusiasm, a consecration to natural truth

The God of sunshine and of storms speaks a less equivocal language than the God of revelation

Our fathers had their religion and their fathers had theirs, but they were not ours, and could not be in those days and under those conditions But their religions lifted them above themselves, they healed

6

their wounds, they consoled them for many of the failures and disappointments of this world, they developed character, they tempered the steel in their nature How childish to us seems the plan of salvation, as our fathers found it in the fervid and, I freely say, inspired utterances of Saint Paul! But it saved them, it built character, it made life serious, it was an heroic creed which has lost credence in our more knowing and more frivolous age We see how impossible it is, but we do not see the great natural truths upon which it rests

A man is not saved by the truth of the things he believes, but by the truth of his belief—its sincerity, its harmony with his character The absurdities of the popular religions do not matter, what matters is the lukewarm belief, the empty forms, the shallow conceptions of life and duty We are prone to think that if the creed is false, the religion is false Religion is an emotion, an inspiration, a feeling of the Infinite, and may have its root in any creed or in no creed What can be more unphilosophical than the doctrines of the Christian Scientists? Yet Christian Science is a good practical religion It makes people cheerful, happy, and helpful—yes, and helps make them healthy too Its keynote is love, and love holds the universe together Any creed that ennobles character and opens a door or a window upon the deeper meanings of this marvelous universe is good enough to live by, and good enough to die by The Japanese-Chinese religion of ancestor worship, sincerely and devoutly held, is better than the veneer of much of our fashionable well-dressed religion

Guided by appearances alone, how surely we should come to look upon the sun as a mere appendage of the earth!—as much so as is the moon How near it seems at sunrise and sunset, and as if these phenomena directly involved the sun, extending to it and modifying its light and heat! We do not realize that these are merely terrestrial phenomena, and that the sun, so to speak, knows them not

Viewed from the sun the earth is a mere speck in the sky, and the amount of the total light and heat from the sun that is received on the earth is so small that the mind can hardly grasp it Yet for all practical purposes the sun shines for us alone Our relation to it could not be any more direct and sustaining if it were created for that purpose It is immanent in the life of the globe It is the source of all our energy and therefore of our life Its bounties are universal The other planets find it is their sun also It is as special and private to them as to us We think the sun paints the bow on the cloud, but the bow follows from the laws of optics The sun knows it not

It is the same with what we call God His bounty is of the same universal, impersonal kind, and yet for all practical purposes it exists especially for us,

8

it is immanent every moment in our lives There is
no special Providence Nature sends the rain upon
the just and the unjust, upon the sea as upon the land
We are here and find life good because Providence
is general and not special The conditions are not
too easy, the struggle has made men of us The bitter
has tempered the sweet Evil has put us on our guard
and keeps us so We pay for what we get

III

That wise old Roman, Marcus Aurelius, says,
"Nothing is evil which is according to nature " At
that moment he is thinking especially of death which,
when it comes in the course of nature, is not an evil,
unless life itself is also an evil After the lamp of
life is burned out, death is not an evil, rather is it a
good But premature death, death by accident or
disease, before a man has done his work or used up
his capital of vitality, is an evil Disease itself is an
evil, but if we lived according to nature there would
be no disease, we should die the natural, painless
death of old age Of course there is no such thing as
absolute evil or absolute good Evil is that which is
against our well-being, and good is that which pro-
motes it We always postulate the existence of life
when we speak of good and evil Excesses in nature
are evil to us because they bring destruction and
death in their train They are disharmonies in the

9

scheme of things, because they frustrate and bring to naught The war which Marcus Aurelius was waging when he wrote those passages was an evil in itself, though good might come out of it

Everything in organic nature—trees, grasses, flowers, insects, fishes, mammals—is beset by evil of some kind The natural order is good because it brought us here and keeps us here, but evil has always dogged our footsteps Leaf-blight is an evil to the tree, smallpox is an evil to man, frost is an evil to the insects, flood an evil to the fishes

Moral evil—hatred, envy, greed, lying, cruelty, cheating—is of another order These vices have no existence below the human sphere We call them evils because they are disharmonies, they are inimical to the highest standard of human happiness and well-being They make a man less a man, they work discord and develop needless friction Sand in the engine of your car and water in the gasoline are evils, and malice and jealousy and selfishness in your heart are analogous evils

In our day we read the problem of Nature and God in a new light, the light of science, or of emancipated human reason, and the old myths mean little to us We accept Nature as we find it, and do not crave the intervention of a God that sits behind and is superior to it The self-activity of the cosmos suffices We accept the tornadoes and earthquakes

and world wars, and do not lose faith We arm ourselves against them as best we can We accept the
bounty of the rain, the sunshine, the soil, the changing seasons, and the vast armory of nonliving forces,
and from them equip or teach ourselves to escape,
endure, modify, or ward off the destructive and
non-human forces that beset our way We draw
our strength from the Nature that seems and is so
regardless of us, our health and wholeness are its
gifts The biologic ages, with all their carnival of
huge and monstrous forms, had our well-being at
heart The evils and dangers that beset our way have
been outmatched by the good and the helpful The
deep-sea fish would burst and die if brought to the
surface, the surface life would be crushed and killed
in the deep sea Life adapts itself to its environment,
hard conditions make it hard Winds, floods, in-
clement seasons, have driven it around the earth,
the severer the cold, the thicker the fur, compensa-
tions always abound If Nature is not all-wise and
all-merciful from our human point of view, she has
placed us in a world where our own wisdom and
mercy can be developed, she has sent us to a school
in which we learn to see her own shortcomings and
imperfections, and to profit by them

The unreasoning, unforeseeing animals suffer more
from the accidents of nature—drought, flood, light-
ning—than man does, but man suffers more from

evils of his own making—war, greed, intemperance, pestilence—so that the development in both lines goes on, and life is still at the flood

Good and evil are inseparable We cannot have light without shade, or warmth without cold, or life without death, or development without struggle The struggle for life, of which Darwinism makes so much, is only the struggle of the chick to get out of the shell, or of the flower to burst its bud, or of the root to penetrate the soil It is not the struggle of battle and hate—the justification of war and usurpation— it is for the most part a beneficent struggle with the environment, in which the fittest of the individual units of a species survive, but in which the strong and the feeble, the great and the small of species alike survive The lamb survives with the lion, the wren with the eagle, the Esquimo with the European—all manner of small and delicate forms survive with the great and robust One species of carnivora, or of rodents, or herbivora, does not, as a rule, exterminate another species It is true that species prey upon species, that cats eat mice, that hawks eat smaller birds, and that man slays and eats the domestic animals Probably man alone has exterminated species But outside of man's doings all the rest belongs to Nature's system of checks and balances, and bears no analogy to human or inhuman wars and conquests

Life struggles with matter, the tree struggles with

the wind and with other trees Man struggles with
gravity, cold, wet, heat, and all the forces that hinder
him The tiniest plant that grows has to force its root
down into the soil, earlier than that it has to burst
its shell or case The corn struggles to lift itself up
after the storm has beaten it down, effort, effort,
everywhere in the organic world Says Whitman
> "Urge and urge and urge,
> Always the procreant urge of the world "

IV

Every few years we have an ice-storm or a snow-
storm that breaks down and disfigures the trees
Some trees suffer much more than others The storm
goes its way, the laws of physical force prevail, the
great world of mechanical forces is let loose upon the
small world of vital forces, occasionally a tree is so
crushed that it never entirely recovers, but after many
years the woods and groves have repaired the damages
and taken on their wonted thrifty appearance The
evil was only temporary, the world of trees has
suffered no permanent set-back But had the trees been
conscious beings, what a deal of suffering they would
have experienced! An analogous visitation to human
communities entails a heritage of misery, but in time
it too is forgotten and its scars healed Fire, blood,
war, epidemics, earthquakes, are such visitations,
but the race survives them and reaps good from them

13

We say that Nature cares nothing for the individual, but only for the race or the species The whole organic world is at war with the inorganic, and as in human wars the individuals are sacrificed that the army, the whole, may live, so in the strife and competition of nature, the separate units fall that the mass may prosper

It is probably true that in the course of the biological history of the earth, whole species have been rendered extinct by parasites, or by changing outward conditions But this has been the exception, and not the rule The chestnut blight now seems to threaten the very existence of this species of tree in this country, but I think the chances are that this fungus will meet with some natural check

In early summer comes the June drop of apples The trees start with more fruit than they can carry, and if they are in vigorous health, they will drop the surplus It is a striking illustration of Nature's methods The tree does its own thinning But if not at the top of its condition, it fails to do this It takes health and strength simply to let go, only a living tree drops its fruit or its leaves, only a growing man drops his outgrown opinions

If we put ourselves in the place of the dropped apples, we must look upon our fate as unmixed evil If we put ourselves in the place of the tree and of the apples that remain on it, the June drop would appear an unmixed good—finer fruit, and a healthier, longer-lived tree results Nature does not work so much to specific as to universal ends The individual may go, but the type must remain The ranks may be decimated, but the army and its cause must triumph Life in all its forms is a warfare only in the sense that it is a struggle with its outward conditions, in which, other things being equal, the strongest force prevails Small and weak forms prevail also, because the competing forms are small and weak, or because at the feast of life there is a place for the small and weak also But lion against lion, man against man, mouse against mouse, the strongest will, in the end, be the victor

Man's effort is to save waste, to reduce friction, to take short cuts, to make smooth the way, to seize the advantage, to economize time, but the physical forces know none of these things

Go into the woods and behold the evil the trees have to contend with—all typical of the evil we have to contend with—too crowded in places, one tree crushing another by its fall, specimens on every hand whose term of life might be lengthened by a little wise surgery, borers, blight, disease, insect pests, storm, wreckage, thunderbolt scars, or destruction—evil in a hundred forms besetting every tree, and sooner or later leaving its mark A few escape—oaks, maples, pines, elms—and reach a

15

greater age than the others, but they fail at last, and when they have rounded out their green century, or ten centuries, and go down in a gale, or in the stillness of a summer night, how often younger trees are marred or crushed by their fall! But come back after many long years, and their places are filled, and all the scars are healed The new generation of trees is feeding upon the accumulations of the old Evil is turned to good The destruction of the cyclone, the ravages of fire, the wreckage of the ice-storm, are all obliterated and the forest-spirit is rank and full again

There is no wholesale exemption from this rule of waste and struggle in this world, nor probably in any other We have life on these terms The organic world develops under pressure from within and from without Rain brings the perils of rain, fire brings the perils of fire, power brings the perils of power The great laws go our way, but they will break us or rend us if we fail to keep step with them Unmixed good is a dream, unmixed happiness is a dream, perfection is a dream, heaven and hell are both dreams of our mixed and struggling lives, the one the outcome of our aspirations for the good, the other the outcome of our fear of evil

The trees in the woods, the plants in the fields encounter hostile forces the year through, storms crash or overthrow them, visible and invisible enemies prey upon them, yet are the fields clothed in verdure and the hills and plains mantled with superb forests Nature's haphazard planting and sowing and her wasteful weeding and trimming do not result in failure as these methods do with us A failure of hers with one form or species results in the success of some other form All successes are hers Allow time enough and the forest returns in the path of the tornado, but maybe with other species of trees The birds and squirrels plant oaks and chestnuts amid the pines and the winds plant pines amid the oaks and chestnuts The robins and the cedar-birds sow the red cedar broadcast over the landscape, and plant the Virginia creeper and the poison-ivy by every stub and fence-post The poison-ivy is a triumph of Nature as truly as is the grapevine or the morning-glory All are hers Man specializes, he selects this or that, selects the wheat and rejects the tares, but Nature generalizes, she has the artist's disinterestedness, all is good, all are parts of her scheme She nourishes the foul-smelling catbrier as carefully as she does the rose Each creature, with man at the head, says, "The world is mine, it was created for me " Evidently it was created for all, at least all forms are at home here Nature's system of checks and balances preserves her working equilibrium If a species of forest worm under some exceptionally favoring conditions gets such a start that it threatens to destroy our beech and maple

17

forests, presently a parasite, stimulated by this turn in its favor, appears and restores the balance For two or three seasons the beech-woods in my native town were ravaged by some kind of worm or beetle, in midsummer the sunlight came into them as if the roof had been taken off, later they swarmed with white millers But the scourge was suddenly checked —some parasite, probably a species of ichneumon-fly, was on hand to curtail the dangerous excess

I am only trying to say that after we have painted Nature as black as the case will allow, after we have depicted her as a savage beast, a devastating storm, a scorching desert, a consuming fire, an all-engulfing earthquake, or as war, pestilence, famine, we have only depicted her from our limited human point of view But even from that point of view the favoring conditions of life are so many, living bodies are so adaptive, the lift of the evolutionary impulse is so unconquerable, the elemental laws and forces are so overwhelmingly on our side, that our position in the universe is still an enviable one "Though he slay me, yet will I trust in him " Slain, I shall nourish some other form of life, and the books will still balance— not my books, but the vast ledgers of the Eternal

In the old times we accounted for creation in the simple terms of the Hebrew Scriptures—"In the beginning God created the heaven and the earth " We even saw no discrepancy in the tradition that

creation took place in the spring But when we at-
tempt to account for creation in the terms of science
or naturalism, the problem is far from being so simple
We have not so tangible a point from which to start
It is as if we were trying to find the end or the beginning of the circle Round and round we go, caught
in the endless and beginningless currents of the Creative Energy, no fixity or finality anywhere, rest and
motion, great and small, up and down, heat and cold,
good and evil, near and far, only relative, cause and
effect merging and losing themselves in each other,
life and death perpetually playing into each other's
hands, interior within interior, depth beneath depth,
height above height, the tangible thrilled and
vibrating with the intangible, the material in bonds
to the non-material, invisible, impalpable forces
streaming around us and through us, perpetual change
and transformation on every hand, every day
a day of creation, every night a revelation of unspeakable grandeur, suns and systems forming in the cy-
clones of stardust, the whole starry host of heaven
flowing like a meadow brook, but where, or whence,
who can tell? The center everywhere, the circum-
ference nowhere, pain and pleasure, good and evil,
inextricably mixed, the fall of man a daily and hourly
occurrence, the redemption of man, the same!
Heaven or hell waiting by every doorstep, bound-
less, beginningless, unspeakable, immeasurable—

what wonder that we seek a short cut through this wilderness and appeal to the supernatural?

When I look forth upon the world and see how, regardless of man and his well-being, the operations of Nature go on—how the winds and the storms wreck him or destroy him, how the drought or the floods bring to naught his industries, how not the least force in heaven or earth turns aside for him, or makes any exception to him, in short, how all forms of life are perpetually ground between the upper and the nether millstones of the contending and clashing natural material forces, I ask myself "Is there nothing, then, under the sun, or beyond the sun, that has a stake in our well-being? Is life purely a game of chance, and is it all luck that we are here in a world so richly endowed to meet all our requirements?" Serene Reason answers "No, it is not luck as in a lottery It is the good fortune of the whole It was inherent in the constitution of the whole, and it continues because of its adaptability, life is here because it fits itself into the scheme of things, it is flexible and compromising" We find the world good to be in because we are adapted to it, and not it to us The vegetable growth upon the rocks where the sea is forever pounding is a type of life, the waves favor its development Life takes advantage of turbulence as well as of quietude, of drought as well as of floods, of deserts as well as of marshes,

of the sea-bottom as well as of the mountain-tops
Both animal and vegetable life trim their sails to the
forces that beat upon them The image of the sail is
a good one Life avails itself of the half-contrary
winds, it captures and imprisons their push in its
sails, by yielding a little, it makes headway in the
teeth of the gale, it gives and takes, without struggle,
without opposition, life would not be life The
sands of the shore do not struggle with the waves,
nor the waves with the sands, the buffeting ends
where it began But trees struggle with the wind,
fish struggle with the flood, man struggles with his
environment, all draw energy from the forces that
oppose them Life gains as it spends, its waste is an
investment Not so with purely material bodies
They are like the clock, they must be perpetually
wound from without A living body is a clock,
perpetually self-wound from within

The faith and composure of the naturalist or
naturist are proof against the worst that Nature can
do He sees the cosmic forces only, he sees nothing
directly mindful of man, but man himself, he sees
the intelligence and beneficence of the universe flowering in man, he sees life as a mysterious issue of the
warring element, he sees human consciousness and
our sense of right and wrong, of truth and justice,
as arising in the evolutionary sequence, and turning
and sitting in judgment upon all things, he sees that

21

there can be no life without pain and death, that
there can be no harmony without discord, that oppo-
sites go hand in hand, that good and evil are inextricably mingled, that the sun and blue sky are still
there behind the clouds, unmindful of them, that all
is right with the world if we extend our vision deep
enough, that the ways of Nature are the ways of God
if we do not make God in our own image, and make
our comfort and well-being the prime object of
Nature Our comfort and well-being are provided
for in the constitution of the world, but we may say
that they are not guaranteed, they are contingent upon
many things, but the chances are upon our side He
that would save his life shall lose it—lose it in for-
getting that the universe is not a close corporation, or
a patented article, and that it exists for other ends
than our own But he who can lose his life in the larger
life of the whole shall save it in a deeper, truer sense

A Free Man's Worship[1]

To Dr Faustus in his study, Mephistopheles told the history of the Creation, saying

"The endless praises of the choirs of angels had begun to grow wearisome, for, after all, did he not deserve their praise? Had he not given them endless joy? Would it not be more amusing to obtain undeserved praise, to be worshipped by beings whom he tortured? He smiled inwardly, and resolved that the great drama should be performed

"For countless ages the hot nebula whirled aimlessly through space At length it began to take shape, the central mass threw off planets, the planets cooled, boiling seas and burning mountains heaved and tossed, from black masses of cloud hot sheets of rain deluged the barely solid crust And now the first germ of life grew in the depths of the ocean, and developed rapidly in the fructifying warmth into vast forest trees, huge ferns springing from the damp mould, sea monsters breeding, fighting, devouring, and passing away And from the monsters, as the play unfolded

[1] Reprinted from the *Independent Review*, December, 1903

itself, Man was born, with the power of thought, the knowledge of good and evil, and the cruel thirst for worship And Man saw that all is passing in this mad, monstrous world, that all is struggling to snatch, at any cost, a few brief moments of life before Death's inexorable decree And Man said 'There is a hidden purpose, could we but fathom it, and the purpose is good, for we must reverence something, and in the visible world there is nothing worthy of reverence ' And Man stood aside from the struggle, resolving that God intended harmony to come out of chaos by human efforts And when he followed the instincts which God had transmitted to him from his ancestry of beasts of prey, he called it Sin, and asked God to forgive him But he doubted whether he could be justly forgiven, until he invented a divine Plan by which God's wrath was to have been ap-peased And seeing the present was bad, he made it yet worse, that thereby the future might be better And he gave God thanks for the strength that en-abled him to forgo even the joys that were possible And God smiled, and when he saw that Man had become perfect in renunciation and worship, he sent another sun through the sky, which crashed into Man's sun, and all returned again to nebula

" 'Yes,' he murmured, 'it was a good play, I will have it performed again ' "

Such, in outline, but even more purposeless, more

24

void of meaning, is the world which Science presents for our belief Amid such a world, if anywhere, our ideals henceforward must find a home That Man is the product of causes which had no prevision of the end they were achieving, that his origin, his growth, his hopes and fears, his loves and his beliefs, are but the outcome of accidental collocations of atoms, that no fire, no heroism, no intensity of thought and feeling, can preserve an individual life beyond the grave, that all the labours of the ages, all the devotion, all the inspiration, all the noonday brightness of human genius, are destined to extinction in the vast death of the solar system, and that the whole temple of Man's achievement must inevitably be buried beneath the debris of a universe in ruins—all these things, if not quite beyond dispute, are yet so nearly certain, that no philosophy which rejects them can hope to stand Only within the scaffolding of these truths, only on the firm foundation of unyielding despair, can the soul's habitation henceforth be safely built

How, in such an alien and inhuman world, can so powerless a creature as Man preserve his aspirations untarnished? A strange mystery it is that Nature, omnipotent but blind, in the revolutions of her secular hurryings through the abysses of space, has brought forth at last a child, subject still to her power, but gifted with sight, with knowledge of good and evil,

25

with the capacity of judging all the works of his unthinking Mother In spite of Death, the mark and seal of the parental control, Man is yet free, during his brief years, to examine, to criticise, to know, and in imagination to create To him alone, in the world with which he is acquainted, this freedom belongs, and in this lies his superiority to the resistless forces that control his outward life

The savage, like ourselves, feels the oppression of his impotence before the powers of Nature, but having in himself nothing that he respects more than Power, he is willing to prostrate himself before his gods, without inquiring whether they are worthy of his worship Pathetic and very terrible is the long history of cruelty and torture, of degradation and human sacrifice, endured in the hope of placating the jealous gods surely, the trembling believer thinks, when what is most precious has been freely given, their lust for blood must be appeased, and more will not be required The religion of Moloch—as such creeds may be generically called— is in essence the cringing submission of the slave, who dare not, even in his heart, allow the thought that his master deserves no adulation Since the independence of ideals is not yet acknowledged, Power may be freely worshipped, and receive an unlimited respect, despite its wanton infliction of pain

But gradually, as morality grows bolder, the claim

of the ideal world begins to be felt, and worship, if it is not to cease, must be given to gods of another kind than those created by the savage Some, though they feel the demands of the ideal, will still consciously reject them, still urging that naked Power is worthy of worship Such is the attitude inculcated in God's answer to Job out of the whirlwind the divine power and knowledge are paraded, but of the divine goodness there is no hint Such also is the attitude of those who, in our own day, base their morality upon the struggle for survival, maintaining that the survivors are necessarily the fittest But others, not content with an answer so repugnant to the moral sense, will adopt the position which we have become accustomed to regard as specially religious, maintaining that, in some hidden manner, the world of fact is really harmonious with the world of ideals Thus Man creates God, all-powerful and all-good, the mystic unity of what is and what should be

But the world of fact, after all, is not good, and, in submitting our judgment to it, there is an element of slavishness from which our thoughts must be purged For in all things it is well to exalt the dignity of Man, by freeing him as far as possible from the tyranny of non-human Power When we have realised that Power is largely bad, that man, with his knowledge of good and evil, is but a helpless atom in a world

27

which has no such knowledge, the choice is again presented to us Shall we worship Force, or shall we worship Goodness? Shall our God exist and be evil, or shall he be recognised as the creation of our own conscience?

The answer to this question is very momentous, and affects profoundly our whole morality The worship of Force, to which Carlyle and Nietzsche and the creed of Militarism have accustomed us, is the result of failure to maintain our own ideals against a hostile universe it is itself a prostrate submission to evil, a sacrifice of our best to Moloch If strength indeed is to be respected, let us respect rather the strength of those who refuse that false "recognition of facts" which fails to recognise that facts are often bad Let us admit that, in the world we know, there are many things that would be better otherwise, and that the ideals to which we do and must adhere are not realised in the realm of matter Let us preserve our respect for truth, for beauty, for the ideal of perfection which life does not permit us to attain, though none of these things meet with the approval of the unconscious universe If Power is bad, as it seems to be, let us reject it from our hearts In this lies Man's true freedom in determination to worship only the God created by our own love of the good, to respect only the heaven which inspires the insight of our best moments In action, in desire, we must submit perpetually to the tyranny of outside forces, but in thought, in aspiration, we are free, free from our fellowmen, free from the petty planet on which our bodies impotently crawl, free even, while we live, from the tyranny of death Let us learn, then, that energy of faith which enables us to live constantly in the vision of the good, and let us descend, in action, into the world of fact, with that vision always before us

When first the opposition of fact and ideal grows fully visible, a spirit of fiery revolt, of fierce hatred of the gods, seems necessary to the assertion of free- dom To defy with Promethean constancy a hostile universe, to keep its evil always in view, always ac- tively hated, to refuse no pain that the malice of Power can invent, appears to be the duty of all who will not bow before the inevitable But indignation is still a bondage, for it compels our thoughts to be occupied with an evil world, and in the fierceness of desire from which rebellion springs there is a kind of self-assertion which it is necessary for the wise to overcome Indignation is a submission of our thoughts, but not of our desires, the Stoic freedom in which wisdom consists is found in the submission of our de- sires, but not of our thoughts From the submission of our desires springs the virtue of resignation, from the freedom of our thoughts springs the whole world of art and philosophy, and the vision of beauty by which, at last, we half reconquer the reluctant world But the vision of beauty is possible only to unfettered contemplation, to thoughts not weighted by the load of eager wishes, and thus Freedom comes only to those who no longer ask of life that it shall yield them any of those personal goods that are subject to the mutations of Time

Although the necessity of renunciation is evidence of the existence of evil, yet Christianity, in preaching it, has shown a wisdom exceeding that of the Promethean philosophy of rebellion It must be admitted that, of the things we desire, some, though they prove impossible, are yet real goods, others, however, as ardently longed for, do not form part of a fully purified ideal The belief that what must be renounced is bad, though sometimes false, is far less often false than untamed passion supposes, and the creed of religion, by providing a reason for proving that it is never false, has been the means of purifying our hopes by the discovery of many austere truths

But there is in resignation a further good element even real goods, when they are unattainable, ought not to be fretfully desired To every man comes, sooner or later, the great renunciation For the young, there is nothing unattainable, a good thing desired with the whole force of a passionate will, and yet impossible, is to them not credible Yet, by death, by illness, by poverty, or by the voice of duty, we must learn, each one of us, that the world was not made for us, and that, however beautiful may be the things we crave, Fate may nevertheless forbid them It is the part of courage, when misfortune comes, to bear without repining the ruin of our hopes, to turn away our thoughts from vain regrets This degree of submission to Power is not only just and right it is the very gate of wisdom

But passive renunciation is not the whole of wisdom, for not by renunciation alone can we build a temple for the worship of our own ideals Haunting foreshadowings of the temple appear in the realm of imagination, in music, in architecture, in the untroubled kingdom of reason, and in the golden sunset magic of lyrics, where beauty shines and glows, remote from the touch of sorrow, remote from the fear of change, remote from the failures and disenchantments of the world of fact In the contemplation of these things the vision of heaven will shape itself in our hearts, giving at once a touchstone to judge the world about us, and an inspiration by which to fashion to our needs whatever is not incapable of serving as a stone in the sacred temple

Except for those rare spirits that are born without sin, there is a cavern of darkness to be traversed before that temple can be entered The gate of the cavern is despair, and its floor is paved with the gravestones of abandoned hopes There Self must die, there the eagerness, the greed of untamed desire must be slain, for only so can the soul be freed from the empire of Fate But out of the cavern the Gate of Renunciation leads again to the daylight of wisdom, by whose radiance a new insight, a new joy, a new tenderness, shine forth to gladden the pilgrim's heart

When, without the bitterness of impotent rebellion, we have learnt both to resign ourselves to the outward rule of Fate and to recognise that the non-human world is unworthy of our worship, it becomes possible at last so to transform and refashion the unconscious universe, so to transmute it in the crucible of imagination, that a new image of shining gold replaces the old idol of clay In all the multiform facts of the world—in the visual shapes of trees and mountains and clouds, in the events of the life of man, even in the very omnipotence of Death—the insight of creative idealism can find the reflection of a beauty which its own thoughts first made In this way mind asserts its subtle mastery over the thoughtless forces of Nature The more evil the material with which it deals, the more thwarting to untrained desire, the greater is its achievement in inducing the reluctant rock to yield up its hidden treasures, the prouder its victory in compelling the opposing forces to swell the pageant of its triumph Of all the arts, Tragedy is the proudest, the most triumphant, for it builds its shining citadel in the very centre of the enemy's

32

country, on the very summit of his highest mountain, from its impregnable watchtowers, his camps and arsenals, his columns and forts, are all revealed, within its walls the free life continues, while the legions of Death and Pain and Despair, and all the servile captains of tyrant Fate, afford the burghers of that dauntless city new spectacles of beauty Happy those sacred ramparts, thrice happy the dwellers on that all-seeing eminence Honour to those brave warriors who, through countless ages of warfare, have preserved for us the priceless heritage of liberty, and have kept undefiled by sacrilegious invaders the home of the unsubdued

But the beauty of Tragedy does but make visible a quality which, in more or less obvious shapes, is present always and everywhere in life In the spectacle of Death, in the endurance of intolerable pain, and in the irrevocableness of a vanished past, there is a sacredness, an overpowering awe, a feeling of the vastness, the depth, the inexhaustible mystery of existence, in which, as by some strange marriage of pain, the sufferer is bound to the world by bonds of sorrow In these moments of insight, we lose all eagerness of temporary desire, all struggling and striving for petty ends, all care for the little trivial things that, to a superficial view, make up the common life of day by day, we see, surrounding the narrow raft illumined by the flickering light of human comradeship, the dark ocean on whose rolling waves we toss for a brief hour, from the great night without, a chill blast breaks in upon our refuge, all the loneliness of humanity amid hostile forces is concentrated upon the individual soul, which must struggle alone, with what of courage it can command, against the whole weight of a universe that cares nothing for its hopes and fears Victory, in this struggle with the powers of darkness, is the true baptism into the glorious company of heroes, the true initiation into the overmastering beauty of human existence From that awful encounter of the soul with the outer world, enunciation, wisdom, and charity are born, and with their birth a new life begins To take into the inmost shrine of the soul the irresistible forces whose puppets we seem to be—Death and change, the irrevocableness of the past, and the powerlessness of man before the blind hurry of the universe from vanity to vanity —to feel these things and know them is to conquer them

This is the reason why the Past has such magical power The beauty of its motionless and silent pictures is like the enchanted purity of late autumn, when the leaves, though one breath would make them fall, still glow against the sky in golden glory The Past does not change or strive, like Duncan, after life's fitful fever it sleeps well, what was eager and grasping, what was petty and transitory, has faded away, the things that were beautiful and eternal shine out of it like stars in the night Its beauty, to a soul not worthy of it, is unendurable, but to a soul which has conquered Fate it is the key of religion

The life of Man, viewed outwardly, is but a small thing in comparison with the forces of Nature The slave is doomed to worship Time and Fate and Death, because they are greater than anything he finds in himself, and because all his thoughts are of things which they devour But, great as they are, to think of them greatly, to feel their passionless splendour, is greater still And such thought makes us free men, we no longer bow before the inevitable in Oriental subjection, but we absorb it, and make it a part of ourselves To abandon the struggle for private happiness, to expel all eagerness of temporary desire, to burn with passion for eternal things—this is emancipation, and this is the free man's worship And this liberation is effected by a contemplation of Fate, for Fate itself is subdued by the mind which leaves nothing to be purged by the purifying fire of Time

United with his fellow-men by the strongest of all ties, the tie of a common doom, the free man finds that a new vision is with him always, shedding over every daily task the light of love The life of Man is a long march through the night, surrounded by invisible foes, tortured by weariness and pain, towards a goal that few can hope to reach, and where none may tarry

35

long One by one, as they march, our comrades vanish from our sight, seized by the silent orders of omnipotent Death Very brief is the time in which we can help them, in which their happiness or misery is decided Be it ours to shed sunshine on their path, to lighten their sorrows by the balm of sympathy, to give them the pure joy of a never-tiring affection, to strengthen failing courage, to instil faith in hours of despair Let us not weigh in grudging scales their merits and demerits, but let us think only of their need—of the sorrows, the difficulties, perhaps the blindnesses, that make the misery of their lives, let us remember that they are fellow-sufferers in the same darkness, actors in the same tragedy with ourselves And so, when their day is over, when their good and their evil have become eternal by the immortality of the past, be it ours to feel that, where they suffered, where they failed, no deed of ours was the cause, but wherever a spark of the divine fire kindled in their hearts, we were ready with encouragement, with sympathy, with brave words in which high courage glowed

Brief and powerless is Man's life, on him and all his race the slow, sure doom falls pitiless and dark Blind to good and evil, reckless of destruction, omnipotent matter rolls on its relentless way, for Man, condemned to-day to lose his dearest, to-morrow himself to pass through the gate of darkness, it remains only to cherish, ere yet the blow falls, the lofty thoughts that ennoble his little day, disdaining the coward terrors of the slave of Fate, to worship at the shrine that his own hands have built, undismayed by the empire of chance, to preserve a mind free from the wanton tyranny that rules his outward life, proudly defiant of the irresistible forces that tolerate, for a moment, his knowledge and his condemnation, to sustain alone, a weary but unyielding Atlas, the world that his own ideals have fashioned despite the trampling march of unconscious power